Did Y

NORTH

A MISCELLANY

Compiled by Julia Skinner

With particular reference to the work of Martin Andrew

THE FRANCIS FRITH COLLECTION

www.francisfrith.com

Based on a book first published in the United Kingdom in 2006 by The Francis Frith Collection®

This edition published exclusively for Bradwell Books in 2013
For trade enquiries see: www.bradwellbooks.com or tel: 0800 834 920
ISBN 978-1-84589-409-2

British Library Cataloguing in Publication Data

Did You Know? Northampton - A Miscellany
Compiled by Julia Skinner
With particular reference to the work of Martin Andrew

The Francis Frith Collection
6 Oakley Business Park,
Wylye Road, Dinton,
Wiltshire SP3 5EU
Tel: +44 (0) 1722 716 376
Email: info@francisfrith.co.uk
www.francisfrith.com

Printed and bound in Malaysia
Contains material sourced from responsibly managed forests

Front Cover: **NORTHAMPTON, GEORGE ROW 1922** 72178p

The colour-tinting is for illustrative purposes only, and is not intended to be historically accurate

CONTENTS

INTRODUCTION

For many centuries boot- and shoe-making were major industries of Northamptonshire. This was influenced by two major factors - lush grassland and extensive forests. The bark of oak trees provided the tanning materials, and the flocks and herds grazing on the Northamptonshire grassland provided the latter. By the early 18th century the town of Northampton had already become a noted supplier of footwear to the army, as well as to civilians and the American colonies. Daniel Defoe commented on Northampton's famous footwear in his 'Complete English Tradesman', published in 1726, when he listed all the English towns which contributed to the making of a suit of clothes:

'If his coat be of woollen-cloth, he has that from Yorkshire; the lining is shalloon from Berkshire; the waistcoat is of callamanco from Norwich; the breeches of a strong drugget from Devizes, Wiltshire; the stockings being of yarn from Westmorland; the hat is a felt from Leicester; the gloves of leather from Somersetshire; the shoes from Northampton; the buttons from Macclesfield in Cheshire, or, if they are of metal, they come from Birmingham, or Warwickshire; his garters from Manchester; his shirt of home-made linen of Lancashire, or Scotland'.

'Brabner's Gazetteer of England and Wales' listed the industries of Northampton in 1895, showing that boot- and shoe-making and the associated trades were still one of the mainstays of Northampton's economy: 'Immense quantities of boots and shoes are still made for the supply of the army, the London market and for exportation. A large trade is also carried on in the tanning and currying of leather. The breweries of Northampton are among the largest in the kingdom, and there are several important maltings and large flour mills. There are also some extensive iron foundries, and bricks and tiles are made to a considerable extent around the town'.

In 1965 it was announced in Parliament that Northampton was to become one of the 'New Towns' to accommodate London's overspill, and in 1968 the Northampton Development Corporation was established. A Master Plan was drawn up and work started on new housing and industrial estates and centres, initially to the east and south of the old town; the aim was to more than double Northampton's population by 1981. The nearby M1 put the expanding town at the hub of the national road network, with direct links to London, Birmingham and the north, and Northampton now has a population of over 200,000.

In the last decades of the 20th century the old town centre of Northampton was subject to much redevelopment, in common with the rest of the country, when many old buildings were demolished and town centres were redeveloped. Northampton before 'modernisation' was a town in which small brick factory buildings and foundries co-existed with shops, offices and houses, and smells wafted over the town from the tanneries and breweries. This was before much of the town's fabric surrendered to the motorcar and lorry, and before the inner ring road turned the old Horse Market, Broad Street and Gas Street into a dual carriageway cutting off Mare Fair from the town centre. Fortunately, the town had enough density of historic buildings to weather the storm with much of its character intact, and enough of Northampton's pre-1960 fabric remains to make the town centre worthy of inspection. There is no doubt that moves such as the pedestrianisation of much of Abington Street and the retention of Market Square as a real market place have helped to give the town back to the people.

The story of Northampton is full of fascinating characters and events, of which this book can only provide a brief glimpse.

NORTHAMPTONSHIRE DIALECT WORDS AND PHRASES

'Clang' - to eat voraciously.

'Cack-handed' - left-handed, which came to mean doing something in an awkward fashion.

'Clod hoppers' - heavy boots.

'Grandad's slippers' - mud on your boots.

'Cod chops' - used to describe someone whose mouth is permanently open.

'Jitty' - an alley, a narrow walk-way between or alongside buildings.

'Peps' - sweets.

'Otch' - move, as in *'Otch up!'* - move up!

'Chopse' - to chat or chatter.

'Me dook' - My dear, a term of endearment.

'Old Frank' - a heron.

'Packup' - a packed lunch.

'Spotting' - starting to rain.

'Knockroad' - awkward.

Northampton's important footwear industry prompted Thomas Fuller (1608-1661) to write that Northampton 'may be said to stand chiefly on other men's legs', and an old saying asserted that 'you know when you are within a mile of Northampton by the smell of the leather and the noise of the lapstones'.

HAUNTED NORTHAMPTON

A former teacher at the Notre Dame Convent School in Abington Street was believed to haunt the building. The ghost was only seen from the knees up, and it was believed that the floor level of the hall that she walked across had been raised since the teacher's death. The school has now been demolished and replaced with shops and offices.

Several of Northampton's pubs are linked with mysterious activity: unexplained footsteps have been heard in the Black Lion, where beer barrels are sometimes moved around by unseen hands. Lights are also turned on and off, and there have been reported sightings of ghostly customers in the building. The Wig and Pen in St Giles Street is also supposed to have a spooky entity in its basement, of which dogs are particularly scared, and the Shipman's is said to be haunted by the ghost of a former manager, Harry Franklin.

The Wheatsheaf Inn is famous for a story in which the ghost of Lord Strafford appeared to Charles I before the Battle of Naseby in 1645; the phantom tried to give the king advice before the battle, but Charles ignored it and his army was defeated (this story is also linked with another pub in Daventry).

A now-demolished house at 18 Horsemarket was said to be haunted over a long period by the ghost of a lady wearing a black lace dress and white gloves.

Like many theatres in the country the Royal Theatre in Northampton has its resident ghost, a 'Grey Lady', who sits in one of the boxes, appears backstage, moves props around and sometimes causes the electric system to play up.

The Grosvenor Shopping Centre is said to be built on the site of an old Franciscan (Grey Friars) monastery, and is believed to be haunted by the ghost of a monk which has been seen by cleaners at the centre after the shops have closed.

NORTHAMPTON MISCELLANY

At the Peace of Wedmore in AD878 between the Danes and the Anglo-Saxon King Alfred, the two sides agreed to split the country into two areas of control. The area where the Danes were allowed to settle was known as the Danelaw, where Danish laws, not Anglo-Saxon, were followed. Northampton was in the Danelaw, and became an important administrative and military town. In the early 10th century, after the Danes of the Danelaw attacked the English kingdoms of the south, Edward the Elder, King Alfred's son and successor, and his sister Ethelfleda, 'the Lady of the Mericans', went on the offensive; their aim was the complete re-conquest of the Danelaw. Northampton was reconquered by Edward, who made it the centre of one of his new 'shires' or counties. Northampton prospered as a river port and trading centre, despite being burnt in 1010 by a Danish army under the command of one Thorkil, and burnt again in 1065 by the rebellious northern earls Edwin and Morcar as part of their revolt against the then Earl of Northumbria, Tostig.

Northampton has a long civic history which pre-dates the first recorded charter in 1189 (during the reign of Richard I, 'the Lionheart') when the burgesses or merchants paid 200 marks to hold their town 'in chief', that is, direct from the king. By the time of William the Conqueror's great survey of the wealth of his new lands in 1086 that came to be known as the Domesday Book, there were 87 royal burgesses holding their tenements direct from the king, as well as 219 holding theirs from other lords, so the town was already large and had its own reeve and bailiffs.

THE RIVER NENE, THE BOATHOUSE 1922 72185

Did You Know?
NORTHAMPTON
A MISCELLANY

ALL SAINTS' CHURCH
1922 72191

The Great Fire of Northampton in 1675 started in a thatched cottage in St Mary's Street, and quickly spread eastwards, fanned by strong westerly winds. The fire consumed three-quarters of the town, including Horse Fair, Market Square and Abington Street. Very little survived the fire, apart from the stone churches and a couple of stone-built houses. One is the Welsh House (of 1595) in Market Square, now restored to its original appearance with its elaborate gabled dormers, and the other is Hazelrigg House in Mare Fair (see photograph 72177 on page 10), which was south-west of the fire and in an area largely untouched by it. The conflagration was described by Daniel Defoe in his 'Tour Through the Whole Island of Great Britain' (1724-27) from an account given by an eye-witness who was standing near the Eleanor Cross at Hardingstone: 'a townsman being at Queen's Cross upon a hill on the south side of the town, about two miles off, saw the fire at one end of the town then newly begun, and that before he could get to the town it was burning at the remotest end, opposite where he first saw it'.

Much of the medieval All Saints' Church was destroyed in the town fire of 1675, though the tower survives from the earlier building, as does the chancel crypt. The church was rebuilt in the classical style, probably designed by Henry Bell from King's Lynn, and was completed in 1680. The medieval tower, formerly a crossing tower, was retained, and a forecourt or square was created in front of the portico on the site of the medieval nave. The cupola on the tower was added in 1704.

In 1215 King John authorised the appointment of William Tilly as the town's first mayor. He also ordered that 'twelve of the better and more discreet' residents of the town should join him as a council to assist in the running of the town. The importance of Northampton at this time is underlined by the fact that London, York and King's Lynn were the only other towns in England which had mayors by this date.

MARKET PLACE 1922 72169

HAZELRIGG HOUSE (OR CROMWELL HOUSE), MARE FAIR 1922 72177

THE GUILDHALL 1922 72181

Hazelrigg House in Mare Fair (see photograph 72177, opposite) was apparently built in 1662 and was bought by Robert Hazelrigg in 1677; it remained in the family until 1835. Now with three round gabled dormers, the house was originally two bays longer. The house is one of only a handful of buildings in Northampton which survived the fire of 1675. There is a local legend of Oliver Cromwell spending the night here before the Battle of Naseby, but this is probably both romantic and fanciful.

In the later Middle Ages the royal connection became less significant to Northampton than it had been in earlier centuries, and by the time of the Civil War in the 17th century the town was decidedly pro-Parliament. Northampton had a long history of religious dissent, from the Lollards of the 15th century onwards, and Puritanism gained a strong hold on the town. The Corporation refused to provide troops to Charles I in 1632 or to pay the notorious Ship Money tax in 1636, and in 1642 petitioned Parliament against papists and bishops.

Northampton's heavily-decorated Guildhall is seen in photograph 72181, opposite. As the photograph demonstrates, it consists of two storeys with a clock tower, a turreted gable and lines of windows. Between the upper windows are pillars with standing statues under canopies. From right to left they represent the Archangel Michael (Northampton's patron saint), Edward IV, Henry VII, Queen Victoria, Edward I, Henry III, Richard I, St George, St Andrew and St Patrick.

Northampton's boot- and shoe-making industry was well established by the time of the Civil War: it is known that over 4,000 pairs of leather shoes and 600 pairs of cavalry jack-boots were made here for the Parliamentary armies during the conflict, and a further 2,000 pairs of boots for Cromwell's New Model Army in 1648.

A medieval hospital, or almshouses, St John's, was founded by William de St Clare about 1138. Part of this hospital still survives, and is situated east of Bridge Street. It was bought in 1877 for a Roman Catholic community; in 1955 the building was converted into a church and the medieval chapel of the hospital became a side chapel to this church.

Photograph N40009, opposite, shows a lost view of Northampton's market place. Every building in this photograph has been demolished, including the grandiose Emporium Arcade of 1901 and the modernistic Mercury and Herald offices to its right. Together with an entire street, Newland (to the right of the Mercury and Herald offices), all were replaced by the 1970s Grosvenor Centre shopping malls. The elaborate fountain in the centre was erected to commemorate the wedding in 1863 of the Prince of Wales (later Edward VII) and the Danish Princess Alexandra; it too was demolished, in 1962, after being declared unsafe.

Photograph 72178, opposite, shows what is now the Northampton and County Club on the right, next to the draper's shop. This was originally Northampton's Infirmary, erected in 1744 as the then first hospital outside London. Built as a 30-bed hospital, the Infirmary was founded by Dr John Stonhouse and the Rev Dr Philip Doddridge, a leading Congregational minister. It soon expanded and in 1770 reached 70 beds. It outgrew the site, and in 1793 moved to the Billing Road, then outside the town in healthier air. The new hospital can be seen in photograph 72183 on page 18. Other hospitals in the town included Northampton General Lunatic Asylum, also on the Billing Road, which opened in 1838; it was to be replaced in 1876 by the County Asylum at Berry Wood.

THE MARKET PLACE c1950 N40009

GEORGE ROW 1922 72178

Three of Northampton's medieval churches survived the Great Fire of Northampton of 1675, and two of them, Holy Sepulchre and St Peter's, are of particular interest. Holy Sepulchre, in the north of the walled town, has a circular nave (see photograph 72198, opposite) whose plan copies that of the Church of the Holy Sepulchre in Jerusalem; it is a direct link with the Crusades, when the Holy Land was the scene of campaigns by knights from western Europe. Simon de Senlis, Earl of Northampton, had himself been a crusader, and founded this most unusual church upon his return from Palestine, at some time between 1100 and 1112. There are very few round churches in England. The church was enlarged with a fine 13th-century chancel and later chapels to its east, and a 14th-century tower and spire added to its west. Equally astonishing, for its sculptural richness, is St Peter's Church, near the castle site (see photograph 72200 on page 36); it dates from around 1170 (built by the grandson of Simon de Senlis, another Simon), and is in the ornate Norman style. The stone carving in this church exudes an almost barbaric air: the capitals are full of curious foliage inhabited by mythical winged creatures, writhing figures and animals, and the arches are a profusion of geometric decoration (see photograph 72203, on pages 34-35). The third surviving medieval church is St Giles's, at the east end of the town, which has a Norman crossing tower with the rest being later medieval.

Northampton's physical situation, where the River Nene cuts through the limestone ridge and turns northwards along its west edge, provided an ideal defensive position, as well as the control over a river crossing where key routes converged from all directions. After the Norman Conquest, the strategic value of the town, virtually in the centre of the kingdom, was recognised by the building of a castle.

THE CHURCH OF THE HOLY SEPULCHRE
1922 72198

There were various monasteries and friaries in medieval Northampton. These included a wealthy Cluniac monastery, St Andrew's Priory, founded by Simon de Senlis around 1100. Although it is long gone, it is commemorated in the names of St Andrew's Street, off Broad Street, and Priory Street. There was also a house of Augustinian canons, St James's Abbey, which stood west of the river, which is commemorated in the name of the area of Northampton known as St James. There were three friaries: a Franciscan friary founded in 1226 is now remembered in the name of Greyfriars Street near the bus station; a Blackfriars (Dominican) friary, founded around 1230, and sited near Horse Market; and a Whitefriars (Carmelite) friary, founded in 1271.

The building of Northampton's Norman castle was undertaken by the town's overlord, Simon de Senlis (or St Lis), about 1086. It was probably originally an earth and timber stockaded construction, which was rebuilt in stone over the next two centuries. The castle was taken over by the king in 1130, and was used as an occasional royal residence.

When the Civil War started, Northampton eagerly became one of the most important Parliamentary garrison towns; its defences were improved, and the former royal castle was used as the garrison headquarters. Oliver Cromwell visited the town in 1645, and General Fairfax marched from Northampton to the Battle of Naseby, where Charles I's Royalist army was decisively defeated.

Northampton's castle is now no longer to be seen, for it suffered not one but two cruel fates: the first was after the Civil War and the Commonwealth, for in 1662 the newly-restored Charles II took vengeance on the pro-Parliamentarian town by ordering the castle to be slighted, so that it would not be of any future military use to rebels against the throne. A fair amount of the castle survived this treatment, only to succumb in the 19th century when the railway station was built across its site in 1879. A plaque commemorates the castle in Chalk Lane, which runs curving north along the course of the castle's eastern moat.

The railway first arrived in Northampton in 1845 as a line from Blisworth Junction to Peterborough. Other lines followed, and the final indignity for Northampton's castle was to have a goods shed and goods yard built over the site of the bailey and keep in 1876, expanding the area lost to Castle Station in 1859.

Northampton is the county town of Northamptonshire, and its shire hall was destroyed in the 1675 fire. The County Hall (seen in photograph 72179, below) was built between 1676 and 1678 on the site of the county gaol, which was rebuilt behind it but was largely demolished in 1930. The Hall was the first public building in Northampton to be constructed after the fire of 1675. Within are the courthouses of the Sessions House.

GEORGE ROW 1922 72179

NORTHAMPTON GENERAL HOSPITAL 1922 72183

PARK AVENUE METHODIST CHURCH c1960 N40064

Northampton's 'new' hospital on the Billing Road replaced the Infirmary on George Row in 1793, 'Erected by Voluntary Subscription', as the plaque informs us. It cost £25,000, with several contractors going bankrupt along the way. Originally built as a 70-bed hospital, it was extended in the 1870s and again after that date, but the original front remains, if somewhat swamped by the later additions. The original three-bay right-hand wing was extended in 1887, and the foundation stone was laid by Prince Albert Victor, one of the sons of Queen Victoria. In 1804 the hospital began the enlightened practice of free smallpox vaccination of out-patients. The bust of Edward VII by George Frampton outside the hospital, seen in photograph 72183, opposite, is still there today. The inscription beside it reads: 'Thoughtful for the care and cure of the sick, he founded the King Edward Hospital Fund and left to the world a noble example of wise philanthropy'.

The areas north of Abington Park, across the Wellingborough Road, north-east of the artisan housing between Abington Park and the town centre, were developed from the late 19th century as superior housing estates with villas and semi-detached houses. Building continued well into the 1920s. New churches were built to serve these suburbs, and one of the most striking is shown in photograph N40064, opposite, the Park Avenue Methodist Church. This was a typical design by George Baines & Son, and dates from 1924. These architects had a prolific practice building Nonconformist churches in a late Gothic style, usually in hard red brick with stone dressings, as here. A Baines church usually had a particularly handsome tower, as this one does.

During Henry II's reign the town was host to the council that arraigned Thomas Becket, the Archbishop of Canterbury and Henry's one-time friend and chancellor. Thomas Becket was a great disappointment to the king, who had hoped that he would be a willing ally in bringing the Church under royal control. He was wrong, and Becket was arraigned in Northampton Castle in 1164.

After his trial for treason at Northampton in 1164, Thomas Becket escaped from St Andrew's Priory. By an ancient tradition, he is supposed to have stopped at a well on the Bedford Road for a drink before continuing on his way, eventually taking ship for France and exile. He later returned to England, and was famously martyred in Canterbury Cathedral in 1170, when he was murdered by four knights who may have taken Henry II's angry outburst 'Will no one rid me of this turbulent priest!' a little too literally - or so the king later claimed. The well, marked on the 1610 John Speed map of Northampton, had its well-house rebuilt by the Corporation in 1843 in Gothic style, as seen in photograph 72190, opposite.

Photograph 72168, opposite, shows the fine monument to Lieutenant-Colonel Edgar Mobbs DSO in its original position in Market Square - it was moved to Abington Square in 1931, where it joined another war memorial. Mobbs was a noted Midlands sportsman (see more information on page 44). He enlisted as a private during the First World War, and rose through the ranks to command the 7th Battalion of the Northamptonshire Regiment. He was killed in action in the Ypres Salient on 31 July 1917 at the age of 35, leading men from the Sportsman's Battalion, the 7th (Service) Battalion of the Northamptonshire Regiment, against a concealed German machine gun post at Passchendale. As well as bearing his bust, the monument also depicts sporting and battle scenes. Crowning the pedestal is a bronze figure carrying a torch and wreath in memory of Lieutenant-Colonel Mobbs.

Northampton witnessed many important events during the Middle Ages. It held both the forerunner of parliament (which was more of a great royal council) and full parliaments, before these finally settled in the royal palace of Westminster after following the king around the country. The royal council first met in Northampton from King Stephen's reign (1135-54). The first parliament attended by burgesses or merchants, the forerunners of the later members of the House of Commons, was held at Northampton in 1179. After the Barons' Wars of the 1260s, when the town was besieged and captured from Simon de Montfort, the barons' leader, several parliaments were held here, including the notorious one of 1380 when the first poll tax was passed. This nationally-hated measure provoked the Peasants' Revolt of the following year.

THE MARKET PLACE AND
THE MOBBS MEMORIAL
1922 72168

**ABINGTON STREET AND NOTRE DAME
SCHOOL 1922** 72172

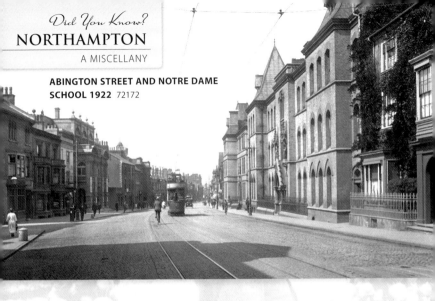

The Northampton Street Tramways Company was founded in 1880.
The horse-drawn trams were a great success, and this improved
transport service encouraged people to move into the new suburbs
around the town. In 1902 the council exercised its option to buy
the tramway system, which then went from strength to strength; it
was extended further into the suburbs, both east and west of the
town. The horse-cars were replaced by electric trams in 1904. The
new motive power allowed larger vehicles, and was surprisingly
profitable. Photograph 72172, above, shows the overhead electricity
supply lines, and a tramcar passing the forbidding brickwork of Notre
Dame School, a school and convent run by the Sisters of Notre Dame
de Namur. Photograph 72176 on page 26 shows the cable support
standards with their metal scrollwork supporting the cable arms.
The tramway system was gradually replaced by motor-buses, and
finally ceased to run in 1934. The motor-buses were introduced in
1923 and initially appeared on routes where trams could not easily
be provided, and rapidly became popular. To the passenger, their
pneumatic tyres and upholstered seats were infinitely preferable to
the rattletrap trams with their plain wooden benches.

When Edward I's beloved wife Eleanor of Castile died at Harby in Nottinghamshire in 1290, the distraught king had elaborate crosses erected at the twelve places where the coffin of his 'chere reine', or 'dear queen', rested overnight on the journey from Nottinghamshire to London (this was the origin of the name of the final resting place, Charing Cross in London). Three of these 'Eleanor Crosses' survive, including the cross that was erected at Hardingstone, which is shown in photograph 72189, below. This was built in 1291 by John of Battle; the statues on it were carved by William of Ireland. The monument is situated on a hill west of Delapré Abbey; the cross on the top had already been broken off by 1460, when the site was described as 'The Hill of the Headless Cross'. It was near collapse at the beginning of the 18th century and was restored in 1713, and again in 1840. It is an important landmark on the London road.

THE QUEEN ELEANOR CROSS 1922 72189

THE MARKET PLACE c1950 N40008

HAZELRIGG HOUSE AND MARE FAIR 1922 72176

'Brabner's Gazetteer of England and Wales' in 1895 described the effect of the 1675 fire and the appearance of 19th-century Northampton thus: 'A fire consumed 600 houses and one of the churches in 1675. The desolation … affected the greater part of the town, made an easy prey of the houses in consequence of their being chiefly built of wood and covered with thatch, and destroyed property estimated at £150,000 in value, but it led to the obtaining an Act of Parliament for rebuilding the town, and occasioned it to be transformed from a state of meanness to a state of comparative beauty.' The speed with which the Act of Parliament for the rebuilding of Northampton was obtained is a reflection of the urgent desire of the Recorder, the then Earl of Northampton, and local merchants and gentry to get the town back on its feet again. Beside the cost being raised by public subscription, the hearth or chimney tax was put towards the work of the rebuilding Commissioners; 10% of the rebuilding money went towards the reconstruction of All Saints' Church, which was the grandest building of the rebuilt town.

Photograph N40008, opposite above, shows the Georgian Peacock Hotel, which was demolished in 1959. Beyond the (surviving) house with the Gothic oriel window is the Welsh House, white-painted and with a shop front, which dates from 1595. It survived the 1675 fire, and was rebuilt in the 1970s, when its long-lost gabled dormers were restored. The name is a reminder of the days when Welsh drovers would bring their cattle to Northampton Market.

After the restoration of the monarchy in 1660, Charles II showed his displeasure with Northampton's support of Parliament during the Civil War not only by ordering the castle and the town walls to be destroyed, but also by purging the Town Corporation. The new council had to pay £200 to have its charter renewed. This revised document required all officials to swear the oath of allegiance, and several office-holders had to have their positions confirmed by the Crown. Nature, however, soon intervened to effect a reconciliation: the Great Fire of 1675 restored harmony, and Charles II even donated timber from the nearby royal forests for the rebuilding of the town.

Medieval Northampton stretched eastwards from the river and castle, with Market Square as its focus. The medieval town walls, demolished as well as the castle at the orders of Charles II in 1662, enclosed about 245 acres (98 hectares), with St Giles's Church near the east gate and the Church of the Holy Sepulchre towards the north gate.

Markets and fairs were a major element in medieval Northampton's trading and manufacturing economy. The first reference to a fair is to one which was held c1180 on All Saints' Day in All Saints' Church and churchyard. In 1235 the fair moved to a waste area north of the church. This waste became the present spacious Market Square, described in 1712 as 'look't upon as the finest in Europe; a fair spacious open place'. The fair grew into an annual event which lasted all of November. The town also acquired various weekly markets, with a charter of 1599 confirming Wednesday, Friday and Saturday as market days. Street names in Northampton give a fair indication of the trades and market centres in the town, for example, Corn Hill, Malt Hill, Mercers Row, Sheep Street and Horse Fair. Market tolls were a major source of the town's income, and market rights were jealously protected, hence the numerous charters obtained over the centuries.

During the First World War, 6,000 men were lost from the Northamptonshire Regiment, of which 1,700 came from Northampton. At the end of the war, the servicemen and women who came home were royally feasted in Abington Park, where trestle tables groaned under the weight of nine roast bullocks, 350 hams, 24,000 pastries and 20,000 pints of beer.

The village of Duston was absorbed into Northampton's borough boundary in 1965. The large factory of British Timken, latterly known as Timken, was east of the village where Main Road curves towards Bants Lane, and employed over 3,000 people in the 1960s (see photograph D202020 on page 37), making bearings and specialist steel castings and fabrications. The factory ceased production in 2002 and the buildings were demolished. The site has now been redeveloped for housing.

DUSTON, MAIN ROAD c1960 D202026

One of the strangest items to be seen in the Northampton Museum and Art Gallery is a huge boot which was worn by an elephant in 1959 when the British Alpine Expedition re-enacted Hannibal's crossing of the Alps with his army and battle elephants in 218BC.

In the medieval period the mayor of Northampton ruled with a council of twelve, later twenty-four, men, and the assembly of the town included all freemen, but by an Act of Parliament of 1469 Northampton and Leicester secured a joint de-democratisation of their town governments. The mayor and ex-mayors, later called aldermen, the twenty-four (the ex-bailiffs) and the forty-eight common councillors made up the closed body that ruled the town until 1835. The 'Forty-Eight' common councillors held office for life, and were replaced by co-option, not election. Not surprisingly, this ruling body became out of touch with the radicalism of the town and its strong Nonconformist and Whig leanings, and was regarded by most townsfolk as an Anglican and Tory preserve. In 1835 the old oligarchic Tory Corporation was reformed, and an elected council replaced it. Town government now alternated between Liberals and Conservatives, with the town achieving independence from Northamptonshire in 1888 when it became a county borough.

THE CHURCH OF THE HOLY
SEPULCHRE 1922 72196

ALL SAINTS' CHURCH, FROM THE EAST c1960 N40058

Northampton's main war memorial was built at the east end of All Saints' churchyard (see photograph N40058, above). It was designed by Sir Edwin Lutyens, who also designed the Cenotaph in Whitehall, and consists of two obelisks with an altar in between. The memorial was unveiled by General Lord Horne on Armistice Day, 11 November, in 1926.

Several street names in Northampton have changed over the years. For instance, The Drapery was once known as The Glovery, reflecting the importance of the gloving industry in the town before it was overshadowed by boot- and shoe-making; and Gold Street was formerly known as Goldsmith Street.

After the fire of 1675, the opportunity for radical re-planning of the town with squares and wider streets was ignored, so the new town arose on a similar street pattern to what had been there before, but without timber-framed houses and thatched roofs. All around the town the charred ruins were swept away, and fine new houses, shops and workshops appeared. The newly-rebuilt Northampton was described in the 1720s by Daniel Defoe as 'the handsomest and best town in all this part of England'.

THE CHURCH OF THE HOLY SEPULCHRE 1922 72195

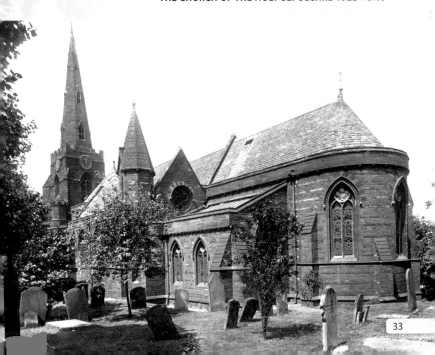

ST PETER'S CHURCH, THE INTERIOR, LOOKING WEST 1922 72203

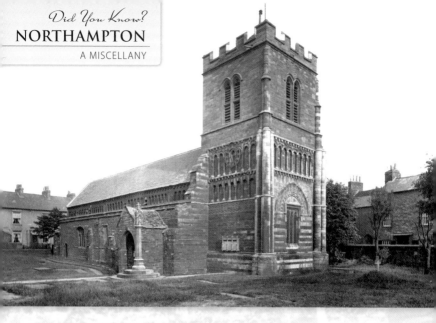

ST PETER'S CHURCH, FROM THE NORTH-EAST 1922 72200

The population of Northampton in 1801 was 7,020, but had jumped to 15,351 by 1831. This increase was probably stimulated by the vast demand for boots for the army during the Napoleonic Wars, creating employment possibilities in the town; a third of the adult males alone in Northampton were shoe-makers in 1831. In the second half of the 19th century the industry rapidly became mechanised, with factories soon becoming the norm, and by 1901 the town's population had expanded to 90,923.

The demand for army boots was virtually insatiable during the First World War, and in 1915 Northampton's factories supplied over 140,000 pairs of boots to the French and Belgian armies alone. During the war the town produced over 23 million pairs of boots for the armed forces.

By the 1860s the Town Corporation was feeling cramped in the 15th-century Guildhall which stood at the south-west corner of Abington Street; as the new Conservative mayor, Christopher Markham, pointed out, it would have long ago been replaced but for the 'great control the ratepayers really exercised over the gentlemen sent there to take care of their pockets'. Following an architectural competition, which was won by Edward Godwin of Bristol, the foundation stone of the new Guildhall in St Giles Square was laid in 1861, and the building formally opened in 1864. Besides council chambers and offices there was a library, which was intended to raise the standards of the local workers' education. The Guildhall was extended in the same style by Matthew Holding in 1889-92, virtually doubling it in width.

DUSTON, BRITISH TIMKEN c1955 D202020

Photograph N40033 shows the Mobbs Memorial in Abington Square, after being moved from Market Square in 1931. Close by, the wall of the 1937 War Memorial Loggia lists the names of Northampton men who fell in the two World Wars. Also seen in this photograph is the statue to Charles Bradlaugh (1833-91), the Northampton freethinker, atheist and, eventually, MP for the town. He was elected in 1880, but refused to swear his oath 'so help me God', and was only allowed to take his seat in 1886.

The custom of concealing shoes in a building, usually in a chimney, was a very old folk custom, and Northampton Museum has set up a Concealed Shoes Index to record all the occurrences throughout the country. It seems that the idea was that the shoes were used as charms to ward off evil spirits who might enter buildings, particularly homes, through their chimneys, and shoes are often found on a ledge or in a specially built cavity in the chimney or behind the hearth. The custom appears to have lasted until well into the 19th century.

Abington Park Museum occupies a manor house that was originally medieval but was greatly altered in the 17th and 18th centuries. The original Tudor house at Abington was once the home of William Shakespeare's only surviving grandchild, Elizabeth, who lived there for 20 years with her second husband, Sir John Bernard. Shakespeare's direct line came to an end when Elizabeth died, childless, in 1670; she is buried in the nearby church.

ABINGTON SQUARE AND THE MOBBS MEMORIAL c1955 N40033

MERCERS ROW c1950 N40001

The common fields of Northampton were enclosed in the 1780s; the commons were retained and vested in the Corporation. These included the Race Course, now Race Course Recreation Ground, Cow Meadow, and other meadows along the River Nene valley. The west part of Cow Meadow was built over as the old cattle market in the 1870s, which has now been replaced. Cow Meadow had a dual purpose as far back as 1703, when pleasure walks were laid out and avenues of trees planted. A chalybeate spring here raised hopes of Northampton aping Bath or Buxton as a spa town, and in 1784 a new walk was laid out from Becket's Well to this spring, Vigo Well - fences were erected to separate customers of quality from the cows. Cow Meadow was renamed Becket's Park in rather grander style, and is now one of the town's best parks, with the River Nene along its south side.

The Drapery and Mercers Row are street names which recall Northampton's historical connection with the textile industry. In the Middle Ages the cloth and wool industries were very important, but had declined by the late Tudor period. By 1600, leather-working was pre-eminent, with glove-making at this point as important as shoe-making. By the late 17th century, boot- and shoe-making had taken precedence, no doubt assisted by the Civil War armies' need for boots and shoes rather than gloves. Until well into the 19th century the shoes were produced in small workshops, often at the bottom of leather-workers' gardens, or in their homes. Separate trades were established for the various processes, from cutting the leather to sewing and soling.

14 miles north of Northampton, close to the A14, is the site of the Battle of Naseby. This battle, which took place in 1645, is considered to be one of the most important engagements of the Civil War, the point at which the tide of war turned against Charles I and in favour of Parliament, ultimately securing the future of Parliamentary democracy. Until this battle the Royalist forces had been the superior side in the war, but at Naseby they were decisively beaten by Cromwell's New Model Army. A monument on the battlefield marks where Cromwell's army gathered to face the Royalists on Dust Hill. The New Model Army was largely formed from existing Parliamentarian armies, and under the leadership of Cromwell it became known for its characteristics of firm discipline and religious and political radicalism. The concept of promotion by merit, not by social rank, was one of its main differences from other armies of the time, and resulted in efficient and capable officers and high morale.

THE MARKET PLACE c1950 N40011

FROM THE TOWER OF ALL SAINTS' CHURCH 1922 72166

The River Nene flows through Northampton, and has been an important trade artery to the town for centuries. One of its key roles was to provide cheap and easy transport when roads were difficult to negotiate. As a result, tanners and shoe-makers set up business along its banks in the earlier medieval period, but in later centuries Northampton's trade declined as towns nearer the sea prospered. It was not until the canal age that Northampton again had good water routes for its trade. The Grand Junction Canal reached the town in 1815 as a branch from Gayton Junction. In a mere five miles it has no less than 17 locks, and merges with the Nene Navigation.

Northampton's General Lunatic Asylum on the Billing Road (renamed St Andrew's Hospital in 1887) was where the rustic labourer poet John Clare ended his days in 1864. Born in 1793, he was the son of a Northamptonshire labourer, and although he had almost no formal education he began writing poetry from the age of 12. In 1820 Clare's first book, 'Poems Descriptive of Rural Life', was well received, but his later volumes failed to sell, and Clare's large family fell into poverty. In 1841, after years of hardship, John Clare went insane and had to be confined in the asylum at Northampton, where he spent the last 23 years of his life. In a lucid moment he once wrote to a friend: 'If life had a second edition, how I would correct the proofs'. He was sometimes referred to as 'the Northamptonshire Peasant Poet', and his sensitive poems describing the beauty of the countryside have remained popular.

A Spring Morning – John Clare

The spring comes in with all her hues and smells,
In freshness breathing over hills and dells;
O'er woods where May her gorgeous drapery flings,
And meads washed fragrant by their laughing springs.
Fresh as new opened flowers untouched and free
From the bold rifling of the amorous bee.
The happy time of singing birds is come,
And love's lone pilgrimage now finds a home;
Amongst the mossy oaks now coos the dove,
And the hoarse crow finds softer notes for love.
The foxes play around their dens, and bark
In joy's excess, 'mid woodland shadows dark;
The flowers join lips below; the leaves above;
And every sound that meets the ear is love.

SPORTING NORTHAMPTON

The Mobbs Memorial in Abington Square commemorates a local sporting and war hero, Lieutenant Colonel Edgar Mobbs DSO, who was killed in the First World War. This remarkable man had been captain of Northampton (Rugby) Football Club, 'the Saints', from 1907 to 1913, and had played seven times for England. He is commemorated each year by the Mobbs Memorial Match between East Midlands and the Barbarians, which was first played in 1921, and is preceded by a wreath-laying ceremony at the Mobbs Memorial. Proceeds from the match go towards the Mobbs Memorial Fund, which assists East Midlands rugby clubs with youth development.

In a county of famous cricketers, Charles Studd and his brothers are as notable as any. They came from the village of Spratton, just outside Northampton, and were a remarkable cricketing family. Charles and two of his brothers captained Cambridge University, the three brothers having this honour in successive years. Charles went on to play in the very first 'Ashes' Test Match. After 1884 he gave up cricket, and became a dedicated missionary in China and Africa.

Northampton Town FC had an extraordinary decade in the 1960s. The club rose from Division Four in 1961 to Division One, only to fall all the way back down by 1969. Northampton Town spent a solitary season in the top flight, but just reaching the top level was a fine achievement. In the great promotion years of 1964-65, goalkeeper Bryan Harvey saved 7 penalties, an incredible record. During the club's season at the top, Northampton Town did the 'double' over Aston Villa, winning at home and away. The clubs have never met in another League match, and Northampton Town thus have a 100% win record over one of the country's most famous clubs.

One of Northampton Town FC's most famous players is the entertainer Des O'Connor. Born in London, he was evacuated to the town during the Second World War, and was a professional on Town's books for a while. He still follows the club's fortunes closely.

Northampton County Cricket Club has been based at the county ground in the town since the 1880s, on a site which for many years adjoined the football ground. The ground staged the first women's Test Match between England and Australia in 1931.

THE RIVER NENE 1922 72187

QUIZ QUESTIONS

Answers on page 50.

1. What is the link between Northampton and the first President of the United States of America?

2. What was Northampton's Town Clerk describing with these words: 'The wind was very strong to blow ye fire on, but it was God who blew ye bellows'?

3. Why is there a statue of Charles II (in Roman costume) above the portico of All Saints' Church?

4. What is the nickname of Northampton Town Football Club?

5. In 1810 a chemist called Philadelphius Jeyes opened a shop in The Drapery. He invented something which is still in use today - what is it?

6. Where in Northampton will you find the autograph of the Royal Ballet's prima ballerina, Dame Margot Fonteyn?

7. When and where was the second Battle of Northampton fought?

8. The Treaty of Northampton was signed in 1328 - why was it important?

9. The first recorded reference to a shoe-maker in Northampton occurs in 1202. What was his name?

10. What is the link between Northampton and a unique political assassination in British history?

RECIPE

NORTHAMPTONSHIRE PUDDING

Ingredients

110g/4oz plain flour	2 eggs
75g/3oz caster sugar	2 tablespoonfuls raspberry
50g/2oz butter or margarine	jam

Sieve the flour. Cream the butter or margarine and sugar together until light and fluffy, and gradually beat in the eggs, adding a tablespoonful of flour to prevent the mixture curdling. Fold in the remaining flour, and stir in one tablespoonful of the jam. Place the remaining jam in the bottom of a greased pudding basin, and pour the pudding mixture into the basin. Cover with pleated greaseproof paper and foil. Place the pudding basin in a large saucepan of boiling water and steam for about 2 hours, topping up the water with more boiling water when necessary. When cooked, turn out on to a serving dish, and serve hot with custard or cream.

RECIPE

NORTHAMPTONSHIRE CHEESECAKES
Small cheesecakes were traditionally made in Northamptonshire to be eaten at sheep-shearing time.

Ingredients
225g/8oz shortcrust pastry
175g/6oz curd cheese or cream cheese
50g/2oz butter or margarine
2 eggs
75g/3oz caster sugar

115g/4oz currants
Finely grated rind of 1 lemon
¼ teaspoonful almond essence
½ teaspoonful ground nutmeg

Preheat the oven to 180 degrees C/350 degrees F/Gas Mark 4.

Roll out the pastry on a lightly floured surface, and use it to line 14-16 lightly greased patty tins. In a bowl, beat the curd or cream cheese until it is smooth. Put the butter or margarine, eggs and sugar into a saucepan and heat gently, stirring all the time, until the mixture has thickened - be careful not to allow it to boil. Remove the pan from the heat, and stir in the curd or cream cheese, the currants, lemon rind and almond essence, making sure that the ingredients are well combined. Fill the patty tins with the mixture, dust the cheesecakes with a little ground nutmeg and bake for 20-25 minutes until well risen. Serve hot or cold.

QUIZ ANSWERS

1. George Washington, the first President of the United States of America, was a direct descendant of Lawrence Washington, who was twice Mayor of Northampton. Lawrence Washington bought Sulgrave Manor, a few miles south-west of Northampton just off the B4525, from Henry VIII at the Dissolution of the Monasteries; it remained in the family until 1610. Sulgrave Manor is now a museum, much visited by American tourists. The Washington coat of arms, which can be seen above the porch of Sulgrave Manor, is thought to have been the basis for the Stars and Stripes flag of the USA.

2. The Town Clerk was describing the winds which were fanning the Great Fire of Northampton of 1675; this disaster destroyed much of the historic heart of the old town.

3. The statue of Charles II was set above the portico of All Saints' Church in 1712, in gratitude for his gift of 1,000 tons of timber towards the rebuilding of the church after the town fire of 1675.

4. The Cobblers. Northampton Town Football Club acquired this nickname soon after its formation in 1897, as over 40% of the town's population was employed in the boot- and shoe-making trade at that time.

5. Philadelphius Jeyes was the formulator of Jeyes Fluid, the well-known antiseptic and disinfectant.

6. In the Central Museum and Art Gallery, which holds a fascinating collection of footwear through the ages, considered to be the finest of its kind in the world. The museum holds a number of boots, shoes and slippers that were worn and donated by famous people. One of the exhibits is a peach satin ballet shoe worn by Dame Margot Fonteyn, which is autographed by her. Amongst many other items of interest in the museum are the shoes that Queen Victoria wore at her wedding.

7. The second Battle of Northampton was a crucial battle of the Wars of the Roses, at which the Yorkists captured the king, Henry VI. The battle was fought at Hardingstone Fields on 10 July 1460, between the Yorkists, led by the Earl of Warwick, and the Lancastrians, commanded by the Duke of Buckingham. When the Yorkists attacked at 7 o'clock in the morning, the Lancastrian gunners found that their powder had been soaked by rain, and one wing of the Lancastrian army fled the field. As the Yorkist forces advanced, the Earl of Warwick cried out to his soldiers to 'Kill the knights and spare the common soldiers'. The Duke of Buckingham was found dead in front of the king's tent; Henry was seized by his enemies and spent his first night in captivity next to the battlefield. (The first Battle of Northampton took place at the site of Northampton Castle in 1264, when the forces of Henry III over-ran the supporters of Simon de Montfort.)

8. The Treaty of Northampton, which was signed in May 1328, was a peace treaty between the English and the Scots. By the terms of this treaty the English, under Edward III, finally recognised the authority of Robert the Bruce as King of Scotland, and Bruce's infant son was betrothed to the king's sister, Joanna.

9. The first known Northampton shoe-maker was recorded in 1202 as 'Peter the Cordwainer'.

10. The only Prime Minister in British history to have been assassinated was Spencer Perceval, who was shot in the lobby of the House of Commons by John Bellingham in 1812. Spencer Perceval was also Northampton's MP.

FRANCIS FRITH

PIONEER VICTORIAN PHOTOGRAPHER

Francis Frith, founder of the world-famous photographic archive, was a complex and multi-talented man. A devout Quaker and a highly successful Victorian businessman, he was philosophical by nature and pioneering in outlook. By 1855 he had already established a wholesale grocery business in Liverpool, and sold it for the astonishing sum of £200,000, which is the equivalent today of over £15,000,000. Now in his thirties, and captivated by the new science of photography, Frith set out on a series of pioneering journeys up the Nile and to the Near East.

INTRIGUE AND EXPLORATION

He was the first photographer to venture beyond the sixth cataract of the Nile. Africa was still the mysterious 'Dark Continent', and Stanley and Livingstone's historic meeting was a decade into the future. The conditions for picture taking confound belief. He laboured for hours in his wicker dark-room in the sweltering heat of the desert, while the volatile chemicals fizzed dangerously in their trays. Back in London he exhibited his photographs and was 'rapturously cheered' by members of the Royal Society. His reputation as a photographer was made overnight.

VENTURE OF A LIFE-TIME

By the 1870s the railways had threaded their way across the country, and Bank Holidays and half-day Saturdays had been made obligatory by Act of Parliament. All of a sudden the working man and his family were able to enjoy days out, take holidays, and see a little more of the world.

With typical business acumen, Francis Frith foresaw that these new tourists would enjoy having souvenirs to commemorate their days out. For the next thirty years he travelled the country by train and by pony and trap, producing fine photographs of seaside resorts and beauty spots that were keenly bought by millions of Victorians. These prints were painstakingly pasted into family albums and pored over during the dark nights of winter, rekindling precious memories of summer excursions. Frith's studio was soon supplying retail shops all over the country, and by 1890 F Frith & Co had become the greatest specialist photographic publishing company in the world, with over 2,000 sales outlets, and pioneered the picture postcard.

FRANCIS FRITH'S LEGACY

Francis Frith had died in 1898 at his villa in Cannes, his great project still growing. By 1970 the archive he created contained over a third of a million pictures showing 7,000 British towns and villages.

Frith's legacy to us today is of immense significance and value, for the magnificent archive of evocative photographs he created provides a unique record of change in the cities, towns and villages throughout Britain over a century and more. Frith and his fellow studio photographers revisited locations many times down the years to update their views, compiling for us an enthralling and colourful pageant of British life and character.

We are fortunate that Frith was dedicated to recording the minutiae of everyday life. For it is this sheer wealth of visual data, the painstaking chronicle of changes in dress, transport, street layouts, buildings, housing and landscape that captivates us so much today, offering us a powerful link with the past and with the lives of our ancestors.

Computers have now made it possible for Frith's many thousands of images to be accessed almost instantly. The archive offers every one of us an opportunity to examine the places where we and our families have lived and worked down the years. Its images, depicting our shared past, are now bringing pleasure and enlightenment to millions around the world a century and more after his death.

For further information visit: www.francisfrith.com

INTERIOR DECORATION

Frith's photographs can be seen framed and as giant wall murals in thousands of pubs, restaurants, hotels, banks, retail stores and other public buildings throughout Britain. These provide interesting and attractive décor, generating strong local interest and acting as a powerful reminder of gentler days in our increasingly busy and frenetic world.

FRITH PRODUCTS

All Frith photographs are available as prints and posters in a variety of different sizes and styles. In the UK we also offer a range of other gift and stationery products illustrated with Frith photographs, although many of these are not available for delivery outside the UK – see our web site for more information on the products available for delivery in your country.

THE INTERNET

Over 100,000 photographs of Britain can be viewed and purchased on the Frith web site. The web site also includes memories and reminiscences contributed by our customers, who have personal knowledge of localities and of the people and properties depicted in Frith photographs. If you wish to learn more about a specific town or village you may find these reminiscences fascinating to browse. Why not add your own comments if you think they would be of interest to others? See **www.francisfrith.com**

PLEASE HELP US BRING FRITH'S PHOTOGRAPHS TO LIFE

Our authors do their best to recount the history of the places they write about. They give insights into how particular towns and villages developed, they describe the architecture of streets and buildings, and they discuss the lives of famous people who lived there. But however knowledgeable our authors are, the story they tell is necessarily incomplete.

Frith's photographs are so much more than plain historical documents. They are living proofs of the flow of human life down the generations. They show real people at real moments in history; and each of those people is the son or daughter of someone, the brother or sister, aunt or uncle, grandfather or grandmother of someone else. All of them lived, worked and played in the streets depicted in Frith's photographs.

We would be grateful if you would give us your insights into the places shown in our photographs: the streets and buildings, the shops, businesses and industries. Post your memories of life in those streets on the Frith website: what it was like growing up there, who ran the local shop and what shopping was like years ago; if your workplace is shown tell us about your working day and what the building is used for now. Read other visitors' memories and reconnect with your shared local history and heritage. With your help more and more Frith photographs can be brought to life, and vital memories preserved for posterity, and for the benefit of historians in the future.

Wherever possible, we will try to include some of your comments in future editions of our books. Moreover, if you spot errors in dates, titles or other facts, please let us know, because our archive records are not always completely accurate—they rely on 140 years of human endeavour and hand-compiled records. You can email us using the contact form on the website.

Thank you!

For further information, trade, or author enquiries
please contact us at the address below:

The Francis Frith Collection, Unit 6, Oakley Business Park, Wylye Road, Dinton, Wiltshire SP3 5EU.
Tel: +44 (0)1722 716 376 Fax: +44 (0)1722 716 881
e-mail: sales@francisfrith.co.uk **www.francisfrith.com**